Gastronomic Adventures

Flourish in the Kitchen

By

Esther D. Decker

How to choose Flesh.

BEEF. The large stall fed ox beef is the best, it has a coarse open grain, and oily smoothness; dent it with your finger and it will immediately rise again; if old, it will be rough and spungy, and the dent remain.

Cow Beef is less boned, and generally more tender and juicy than the ox, in America, which is used to labor.

Of almost every species of Animals, Birds and Fishes, the female is the tenderest, the richest flavour'd, and among poultry the soonest fattened.

Mutton, grass-fed, is good two or three years old.

Lamb, if under six months is rich, and no danger of imposition; it may be known by its size, in distinguishing either.

Veal, is soon lost—great care therefore is necessary in purchasing. Veal bro't to market in panniers, or in carriages, is to be preferred to that bro't in bags, and flouncing on a sweaty horse.

Pork, is known by its size, and whether properly fattened by its appearance.

To make the best Bacon.

To each ham put one ounce saltpeter, one pint bay salt, one pint molasses, shake together 6 or 8 weeks, or when a large quantity is together, baste them with the liquor every day; when taken out to dry, smoke three weeks with cobs or malt fumes. To every ham may be added a cheek, if you stow away a barrel and not alter the composition, some add a shoulder. For transportation or exportation, double the period of smoking.

Fish, how to choose the best in market.

Salmon, the noblest and richest fish taken in fresh water—the largest are the best. They are unlike almost every other fish, are ameliorated by being 3 or 4 days out of water, if kept from heat and the moon, which has much more injurious effect than the sun.

In all great fish-markets, great fish-mongers strictly examine the gills—if the bright redness is exchanged for a low brown, they are stale; but when live fish are bro't flouncing into market, you have only to elect the kind most agreeable to your palate and the season.

Shad, contrary to the generally received opinion are not so much richer flavored, as they are harder when first taken out of the water; opinions vary respecting them. I have tasted Shad thirty or forty miles from the place where caught, and really conceived that they had a richness of flavor, which did not appertain to those taken fresh and cooked immediately, and have proved both at the same table, and the truth may rest here, that a Shad 36 or 48 hours out of water, may not cook so hard and solid, and be esteemed so elegant, yet give a higher relished flavor to the taste.

Every species generally of *salt water Fish,* are best fresh from the water, tho' the *Hannah Hill, Black Fish, Lobster, Oyster, Flounder, Bass, Cod, Haddock,* and *Eel,* with many others, may be transported by land many miles, find a good market, and retain a good relish; but as generally, live ones are bought first, deceits are used to give them a freshness of appearance, such as peppering the gills, wetting the fins and tails, and even painting the gills, or wetting with animal blood. Experience and attention will dictate the choice of the best. Fresh gills, full bright eyes, moist fins and tails, are denotements of their being fresh caught; if they are soft, its certain they are stale, but if deceits are used, your smell must approve or denounce them, and be your safest guide.

Of all fresh water fish, there are none that require, or so well afford haste in cookery, as the *Salmon Trout,* they are best when caught under a fall or cataract—from what philosophical circumstance is yet unsettled, yet true it is, that at the foot of a fall the waters are much colder than at the head; Trout choose those waters; if taken from them and hurried into dress, they are genuinely good; and take rank in point of superiority of flavor, of most other fish.

Perch and Roach, are noble pan fish, the deeper the water from whence taken, the finer are their flavors; if taken from shallow water, with muddy bottoms, they are impregnated therewith, and are unsavory.

Eels, though taken from muddy bottoms, are best to jump in the pan.

Most white or soft fish are best bloated, which is done by salting, peppering, and drying in the sun, and in a chimney; after 30 or 40 hours drying, are best broiled, and moistened with butter, etc.

Poultry—how to choose.

Having before stated that the female in almost every instance, is preferable to the male, and peculiarly so in the *Peacock*, which, tho' beautifully plumaged, is tough, hard, stringy, and untasted, and even indelicious—while the *Pea Hen* is exactly otherwise, and the queen of all birds.

So also in a degree, *Turkey*.

Hen Turkey, is higher and richer flavor'd, easier fattened and plumper—they are no odds in market.

Dunghill Fowls, are from their frequent use, a tolerable proof of the former birds.

Chickens, of either kind are good, and the yellow leg'd the best, and their taste the sweetest.

Capons, if young are good, are known by short spurs and smooth legs.

All birds are known, whether fresh killed or stale, by a tight vent in the former, and a loose open vent if old or stale; their smell denotes their goodness; speckled rough legs denote age, while smooth legs and combs prove them young.

A Goose, if young, the bill will be yellow, and will have but few hairs, the bones will crack easily; but if old, the contrary, the bill will be red, and the pads still redder; the joints stiff and difficultly disjointed; if young, otherwise; choose one not very fleshy on the breast, but fat in the rump.

Ducks, are similar to geese.

Wild Ducks, have redder pads, and smaller than the tame ones, otherwise are like the goose or tame duck, are to be chosen by the same rules.

Wood Cocks, ought to be thick, fat and flesh firm, the nose dry, and throat clear.

Snipes, if young and fat, have full veins under the wing, and are small in the veins, otherwise like the Woodcock.

Partridges, if young, will have black bills, yellowish legs; if old, the legs look bluish; if old or stale, it may be perceived by smelling at their mouths.

Pigeons, young, have light red legs, and the flesh of a colour, and prick easily—old have red legs, blackish in parts, more hairs, plumper and loose vents—so also of grey or green Plover, Black Birds, Thrash, Lark, and wild Fowl in general.

Hares, are white flesh'd and flexible when new and fresh kill'd; if stale, their flesh will have a blackish hue, like old pigeons, if the cleft in her lip spread much, is wide and ragged, she is old; the contrary when young.

Leveret, is like the Hare in every respect, that some are obliged to search for the knob, or small bone on the fore leg or foot, to distinguish them.

Rabbits, the wild are the best, either are good and tender; if old there will be much yellowish fat about the kidneys, the claws long, wool rough, and mixed with grey hairs; if young the reverse. As to their being fresh, judge by the scent, they soon perish, if trap'd or shot, and left in pelt or undressed; their taint is quicker than veal, and the most sickish in nature; and will not, like beef or veal, be purged by fire.

The cultivation of Rabbits would be profitable in America, if the best methods were pursued—they are a very prolific and profitable animal—they are easily cultivated if properly attended, but not otherwise.—A Rabbit's burrow, on which 3,000 dollars may have been expended, might be very profitable; but on the small scale they would be well near market towns—easier bred, and more valuable.

Butter—Tight, waxy, yellow Butter is better than white or crumbly, which soon becomes rancid and frowy. Go into the center of balls or rolls to prove and judge it; if in firkin, the middle is to be preferred, as the sides are frequently distasted by the wood of the firkin—altho' oak and used for years. New pine tubs are ruinous to the butter. To have sweet butter in dog days, and thro' the vegetable seasons, send stone pots to honest, neat, and trusty dairy people, and procure it pack'd down in May, and let them be brought in, in the night, or cool rainy morning, covered with a clean cloth wet in cold water, and partake of no heat from the horse, and set the pots in the coldest part of your cellar, or in the ice house.—Some say that May butter thus preserved, will go into the winter use, better than fall made butter.

Cheese—The red smooth moist coated, and tight pressed, square edged Cheese, are better than white coat, hard rinded, or bilged; the inside should be yellow, and flavored to your taste. Old shelves which have only been wiped down for years, are preferable to scoured and washed shelves. Deceits are used by salt-petering the out side, or colouring with hemlock, cocumberries, or safron, infused into the milk; the taste of either supersedes every possible evasion.

Eggs—Clear, thin shell'd, longest oval and sharp ends are best; to ascertain whether new or stale—hold to the light, if the white is clear, the yolk regularly in the centre, they are good—but if otherwise, they are stale. The best possible method of ascertaining, is to put them into water, if they lie on their bilge, they are *good* and *fresh*—if they bob up an end they are stale, and if they rise they are addled, proved, and of no use.

Potatoes, take rank for universal use, profit and easy acquirement. The smooth skin, known by the name of How's Potato, is the most mealy and richest flavor'd; the yellow rusticoat next best; the red, and red rusticoat are tolerable; and the yellow Spanish have their value—those cultivated from imported seed on sandy or dry loamy lands, are best for table use; tho' the red or either will produce more in rich, loamy, highly manured garden grounds; new lands and a sandy soil, afford the richest flavor'd; and most mealy Potato much depends on the ground on which they grow—more on the species of Potatoes planted—and still more from foreign seeds—and each may be known by attention to connoisseurs; for a good potato comes up in many branches of cookery, as herein after prescribed.—All potatoes should be dug before the rainy seasons in the fall, well dried in the sun, kept from frost and dampness during the winter, in the spring removed from the cellar to a dry loft, and spread thin, and fre-quently stirred and dried, or they will grow and be thereby injured for cookery.

A roast Potato is brought on with roast Beef, a Steak, a Chop, or Fricassee; good boiled with a boiled dish; make an excellent stuffing for a turkey, water or wild fowl; make a good pie, and a good starch for many uses. All potatoes run out, or depreciate in America; a fresh importation of the Spanish might restore them to table use.

It would swell this treatise too much to say everything that is useful, to prepare a good table, but I may be pardoned by observing, that the Irish have preserved a genuine mealy rich Potato, for a century, which takes rank of any known in any other kingdom; and I have heard that they renew their seed by planting and cultivating the *Seed Ball*, which grows on the tine. The manner of their managing it to keep up the excellency of that root, would better suit a treatise on agriculture and gardening than this—and be inserted in a book which would be read by the farmer, instead of his amiable daughter. If no one treats on the subject, it may appear in the next edition.

Onions—The Medeira white is best in market, esteemed softer flavored, and not so fiery, but the high red, round hard onions are the best; if you consult cheapness, the largest are best; if you consult taste and softness, the very smallest are the most delicate, and used at the first tables. Onions grow in the richest, highest cultivated ground, and better and better year after year, on the same ground.

Beets, grow on any ground, but best on loam, or light gravel grounds; the *red* is the richest and best approved; the *white* has a sickish sweetness, which is disliked by many.

Parsnips, are a valuable root, cultivated best in rich old grounds, and doubly deep plowed, *late sown*, they grow thrifty, and are not so prongy; they may be kept anywhere and anyhow, so that they do not grow with heat, or are nipped with frost; if frosted, let them thaw in earth; they are richer flavored when plowed out of the ground in April, having stood out during the winter, tho' they will not last long after, and commonly more sticky and hard in the center.

Carrots, are managed as it respects plowing and rich ground, similarly to Parsnips. The yellow are better than the orange or red; middling siz'd, that is, a foot long and two inches thick at the top end, are better than over grown ones; they are cultivated best with onions, sowed very thin, and mixed with other seeds, while young or six weeks after sown, especially if with onions on true onion ground. They are good with veal cookery, rich in soups excellent with hash, in May and June.

Garlicks, tho' used by the French, are better adapted to the uses of medicine than cookery.

Asparagus—The mode of cultivation belongs to gardening; your business is only to cut and dress, the largest is best, the growth of a day sufficient, six inches long, and cut just above the ground; many cut below the surface, under an idea of getting tender shoots, and preserving the bed; but it enfeebles the root: dig round it and it will be wet with the juices—but if cut above ground, and just as the dew is going off, the sun will either reduce the juice, or send it back to nourish the root—it's an excellent vegetable.

Parsley, of the three kinds, the thickest and branchiest is the best, is sown among onions, or in a bed by itself, may be dried for winter use; tho' a method which I have experienced is much better—In September I dig my roots, procure an old thin stave dry cask, bore holes an inch diameter in every stave, 6 inches asunder round the cask, and up to the top—take first a half bushel of rich garden mold and put into the cask, then run the roots through the staves, leaving the branches outside, press the earth tight about the root within, and thus continue on thro' the respective stories, till the cask is full; it being filled, run an iron bar thro' the center of the dirt in the cask, and fill with water, let stand on the south and east side of a building till frosty night, then remove it, (by slinging a rope round the cask) into the cellar; where, during the winter, I clip with my scissors the fresh parsley, which my neighbors or myself have occasion for; and in the spring transplant the roots in the bed in the garden, or in any unused corner—or let stand upon the wharf, or the wash shed. It's a useful mode of cultivation, and a pleasurably tasted herb, and much used in garnishing viands.

Raddish, Salmon colored is the best, *purple* next best—*white*—*turnip*—each are produced from southern seeds, annually. They grow thriftiest sown among onions. The turnip Raddish will last well through the winter.

Artichokes—The Jerusalem is best, are cultivated like potatoes, (tho' their stocks grow 7 feet high) and may be preserved like the turnip raddish, or pickled—they like.

Horse Raddish, once in the garden, can scarcely ever be totally eradicated; plowing or digging them up with that view, seems at times rather to increase and spread them.

Cucumbers, are of many kinds; the prickly is best for pickles, but generally bitter; the white is difficult to raise and tender; choose the bright green, smooth and proper sized.

Melons—The Water Melons is cultivated on sandy soils only, above latitude 41 1-2, if a stratum of land be dug from a well, it will bring the first year good Water Melons; the red cored are highest flavored; a hard rind proves them ripe.

Muskmelons, are various, the rough skinned is best to eat; the short, round, fair skinn'd, is best for Mangoes.

Lettuce, is of various kinds; the purple spotted leaf is generally the tenderest, and free from bitter—Your taste must guide your market.

Cabbage, requires a page, they are so multifarious. Note, all Cabbages have a higher relish that grow on *new unmatured grounds*; if grown in an old town and on old gardens, they have a rankness, which at times, may be perceived by a fresh air traveler. This observation has been experienced for years—that Cabbages require new ground, more than Turnips.

The Low Dutch, only will do in old gardens.

The *Early Yorkshire*, must have rich soils, they will not answer for winter, they are easily cultivated, and frequently bro't to market in the fall, but will not last the winter.

The *Green Savoy*, with the richest crinkles, is fine and tender; and altho' they do not head like the Dutch or Yorkshire, yet the tenderness of the out leaves is a counterpoise, it will last thro' the winter, and are high flavored.

The *Yellow Savoy*, takes next rank, but will not last so long; all Cabbages will mix, and participate of other species, like Indian Corn; they are culled, best in plants; and a true gardener will, in the plant describe those which will head, and which will not. This is new, but a fact.

The gradations in the Savoy Cabbage are discerned by the leaf; the richest and most scollup'd, and crinkled, and thickest Green Savoy, falls little short of a Cauliflower.

The red and reddest small tight heads, are best for *slaw*, it will not boil well, comes out black or blue, and tinges other things with which it is boiled.

BEANS.

The Clabboard Bean, is easiest cultivated and collected, are good for string beans, will shell—must be poled.

The Windsor Bean, is an earlier, good string, or shell Bean.

Crambury Bean, is rich, but not universally approved equal to the other two.

Frost Bean, is good only to shell.

Six Weeks Bean, is a yellowish Bean, and early bro't forward, and tolerable.

Lazy Bean, is tough, and needs no pole.

English Bean, what *they* denominate the *Horse Bean*, is mealy when young, is profitable, easily cultivated, and may be grown on worn out grounds; as they may be raised by boys, I cannot but recommend the more extensive cultivation of them.

The small White Bean, is best for winter use, and excellent.

Calivanse, are run out, a yellow small bush, a black speck or eye, are tough and tasteless, and little worth in cookery, and scarcely bear exportation.

Peas—Green Peas.

The Crown Imperial, takes rank in point of flavor, they blossom, purple and white on the top of the vines, will run from three to five feet high, should be set in light sandy soil only, or they run too much to vines.

The Crown Pea, is second in richness of flavor.

The Rondeheval, is large and bitterish.

Early Carlton, is produced first in the season—good.

Marrow Fats, green, yellow, and is large, easily cultivated, not equal to others.

Sugar Pea, needs no bush, the pods are tender and good to eat, easily cultivated.

Spanish Manratto, is a rich Pea, requires a strong high bush.

All Peas should be picked *carefully* from the vines as soon as dew is off, shelled and cleaned without water, and boiled immediately; they are thus the richest flavored.

Herbs, useful in Cookery.

Thyme, is good in soups and stuffings.

Sweet Marjoram, is used in Turkeys.

Summer Savory, ditto, and in Sausages and salted Beef, and legs of Pork.

Sage, is used in Cheese and Pork, but not generally approved.

Parsley, good in *soups*, and to *garnish roast Beef*, excellent with bread and butter in the spring.

Penny Royal, is a high aromatic, altho' a spontaneous herb in old ploughed fields, yet might be more generally cultivated in gardens, and used in cookery and medicines.

Sweet Thyme, is most useful and best approved in cookery.

FRUITS.

Pears, There are many different kinds; but the large Bell Pear, sometimes called the Pound Pear, the yellowest is the best, and in the same town they differ essentially.

Hard Winter Pears, are innumerable in their qualities, are good in sauces, and baked.

Harvest and *Summer Pears* are a tolerable dessert, are much improved in this country, as all other fruits are by grafting and innoculation.

Apples, are still more various, yet rigidly retain their own species, and are highly useful in families, and ought to be more universally cultivated, excepting in the compactest cities. There is not a single family but might set a tree in some otherwise useless spot, which might serve the two fold use of shade and fruit; on which 12 or 14 kinds of fruit trees might easily be engrafted, and essentially preserve the orchard from the intrusions of boys, etc. which is too common in America. If the boy who thus planted a tree, and guarded and protected it in a useless corner, and carefully engrafted different fruits, was to be indulged free access into orchards, whilst the neglectful boy was prohibited—how many millions of fruit trees would spring into growth—and what a saving to the union. The net saving would in time extinguish the public debt, and enrich our cookery.

Currants, are easily grown from shoots trimmed off from old bunches, and set carelessly in the ground; they flourish on all soils, and make good jellies—their cultivation ought to be encouraged.

Black Currants, may be cultivated—but until they can be dried, and until sugars are propagated, they are in a degree unprofitable.

Grapes, are natural to the climate; grow spontaneously in every state in the union, and ten degrees north of the line of the union. The *Madeira*,

Lisbon and *Malaga* Grapes, are cultivated in gardens in this country, and are a rich treat or dessert. Trifling attention only is necessary for their ample growth.

Having pointed out the *best methods of judging of the qualities of Viands, Poultry, Fish, Vegetables, etc.* We now present the best approved methods of DRESSING and COOKING them; and to suit all tastes, present the following

RECEIPTS.

To Roast Beef.

THE general rules are, to have a brisk hot fire, to hang down rather than to spit, to baste with salt and water, and one quarter of an hour to every pound of beef, tho' tender beef will require less, while old tough beef will require more roasting; pricking with a fork will determine you whether done or not; rare done is the healthiest and the taste of this age.

Roast Mutton.

If a breast let it be cauled, if a leg, stuffed or not, let it be done more gently than beef, and done more; the chine, saddle or leg require more fire and longer time than the breast, etc. Garnish with scraped horse radish, and serve with potatoes, beans, cauliflowers, water-cresses, or boiled onion, caper sauce, mashed turnip, or lettuce.

Roast Veal.

As it is more tender than beef or mutton, and easily scorched, paper it, especially the fat parts, lay it some distance from the fire a while to heat gently, baste it well; a 15 pound piece requires one hour and a quarter roasting; garnish with green-parsley and sliced lemon.

Roast Lamb.

Lay down to a clear good fire that will not want stirring or altering, baste with butter, dust on flour, baste with the dripping, and before you take it up, add more butter and sprinkle on a little salt and parsley shred fine; send to table with a nice salad, green peas, fresh beans, or a cauliflower, or asparagus.

To stuff a Turkey.

Grate a wheat loaf, one quarter of a pound butter, one quarter of a pound salt pork, finely chopped, 2 eggs, a little sweet marjoram, summer savory, parsley and sage, pepper and salt (if the pork be not sufficient,) fill the bird and sew up.

The same will answer for all Wild Fowl.

Water Fowls require onions.

The same ingredients stuff a *leg of Veal, fresh Pork* or a *loin of Veal*.

To stuff and roast a Turkey, or Fowl.

One pound soft wheat bread, 3 ounces beef suet, 3 eggs, a little sweet thyme, sweet marjoram, pepper and salt, and some add a gill of wine; fill the bird therewith and sew up, hang down to a steady solid fire, basting frequently with salt and water, and roast until a steam emits from the breast, put one third of a pound of butter into the gravy, dust flour over the bird and baste with the gravy; serve up with boiled onions and cranberry-sauce, mangoes, pickles or celery.

2. Others omit the sweet herbs, and add parsley done with potatoes.

3. Boil and mash 3 pints potatoes, wet them with butter, add sweet herbs, pepper, salt, fill and roast as above.

To stuff and roast a Goslin.

Boil the inwards tender, chop them fine, put double quantity of grated bread, 4 ounces butter, pepper, salt, (and sweet herbs if you like) 2 eggs moulded into the stuffing, parboil 4 onions and chop them into the stuffing, add wine, and roast the bird.

The above is a good stuffing for every kind of Water Fowl, which requires onion sauce.

To smother a Fowl in Oysters.

Fill the bird with dry Oysters, and sew up and boil in water just sufficient to cover the bird, salt and season to your taste—when done tender, put into a deep dish and pour over it a pint of stewed oysters, well buttered and peppered, garnish a turkey with sprigs of parsley or leaves of celery: a fowl is best with a parsley sauce.

To stuff a Leg of Veal.

Take one pound of veal, half pound pork (salted,) one pound grated bread, chop all very fine, with a handful of green parsley, pepper it, add 3 ounces butter and 3 eggs, (and sweet herbs if you like them,) cut the leg round like a ham and stab it full of holes, and fill in all the stuffing; then salt and pepper the leg and dust on some flour; if baked in an oven, put into a sauce pan with a little water, if potted, lay some skewers at the bottom of the pot, put in a little water and lay the leg on the skewers, with a gentle fire render it tender, (frequently adding water,) when done take out the leg, put butter in the pot and brown the leg, the gravy in a separate vessel must be thickened and buttered and a spoonful of ketchup added.

To stuff a leg of Pork to bake or roast.

Corn the leg 48 hours and stuff with sausage meat and bake in a hot oven two hours and a half or roast.

To alamode a round of Beef.

To a 14 or 16 pound round of beef, put one ounce salt-peter, 48 hours after stuff it with the following: one and half pound beef, one pound salt pork, two pound grated bread, chop all fine and rub in half pound butter, salt, pepper and cayenne, summer savory, thyme; lay it on skewers in a large pot, over 3 pints hot water (which it must occasionally be supplied with,) the steam of which in 4 or 5 hours will render the round tender if over a moderate fire; when tender, take away the gravy and thicken with flour and butter, and boil, brown the round with butter and flour, adding ketchup and wine to your taste.

To alamode a round.

Take fat pork cut in slices or mince, season it with pepper, salt, sweet marjoram and thyme, cloves, mace and nutmeg, make holes in the beef and stuff it the night before cooked; put some bones across the bottom of the pot to keep from burning, put in one quart Claret wine, one quart water and one onion; lay the round on the bones, cover close and stop it round the top with dough; hang on in the morning and stew gently two hours; turn it, and stop tight and stew two hours more; when done tender, grate a crust of bread on the top and brown it before the fire; scum the gravy and serve in a butter boat, serve it with the residue of the gravy in the dish.

To Dress a Turtle.

Fill a boiler or kettle, with a quantity of water sufficient to scald the callapach and Callapee, the fins, etc. and about 9 o'clock hang up your Turtle by the hind fins, cut of the head and save the blood, take a sharp pointed knife and separate the callapach from the callapee, or the back from the belly part, down to the shoulders, so as to come at the entrails which take out, and clean them, as you would those of any other animal, and throw them into a tub of clean water, taking great care not to break the gall, but to cut it off from the liver and throw it away, then separate each distinctly and put the guts into another vessel, open them with a small pen-knife end to end, wash them clean, and draw them through a woolen cloth, in warm water, to clear away the slime and then put them in clean cold water till they are used with the other part of the entrails, which must be cut up small to be mixed in the baking dishes with the meat; this done, separate the back and belly pieces, entirely cutting away the fore fins by the upper joint, which scald; peel off the loose skin and cut them into small pieces, laying them by themselves, either in another vessel, or on the table, ready to be seasoned; then cut off the meat from the belly part, and clean the back from the lungs, kidneys, etc. and that meat cut into pieces as small as a walnut, laying it likewise by itself; after this you are to scald the back and belly pieces, pulling off the shell from the back, and the yellow skin from the belly, when all will be white and clean, and with the kitchen cleaver cut those up likewise into pieces about the bigness or breadth of a card; put those pieces into clean cold water, wash them and place them in a heap on the table, so that each part may lay by itself; the meat being thus prepared and laid separate for seasoning; mix two third parts of salt or rather more, and one third part of cayenne pepper, black pepper, and a nutmeg, and mace pounded fine, and mixed all together; the quantity, to be proportioned to the size of the Turtle, so that in each dish there may be about three spoonfuls of seasoning to every twelve pound of meat; your meat being thus seasoned, get some sweet herbs, such as thyme, savory, etc. let them be dried and rub'd fine, and having provided some deep dishes to bake it in, which should be of the common brown ware, put in the coarsest part of the meat, put a quarter pound of butter at the bottom of each dish, and then put some of each of the several parcels of meat, so that the dishes may be all alike and have equal portions of the different parts of the Turtle, and between each laying of meat strew a little of the mixture of sweet herbs, fill your dishes within an inch an half, or two inches of the top; boil the blood of the Turtle, and put into it, then lay on forcemeat balls made of veal, highly seasoned with the same seasoning as the Turtle; put in each dish a gill of Madeira Wine, and as much water as it will conveniently hold, then break over it five or six eggs to keep the meat from scorching at the top, and over that shake a handful of shred parsley, to make it look green, when done put your dishes into an oven made hot enough to bake bread, and in an hour and half, or two hours (according to the size of the dishes) it will be sufficiently done.

To dress a Calf's Head. Turtle fashion.

The head and feet being well scalded and cleaned, open the head, taking the brains, wash, pick and cleanse, salt and pepper and parsley them and put by in a cloth; boil the head, feet and heartslet one and quarter, or one and half hour, sever out the bones, cut the skin and meat in slices, strain the liquor in which boiled and put by; clean the pot very clean or it will burn too, make a layer of the slices, which dust with a composition made of black pepper one spoon, of sweet herbs pulverized, two spoons (sweet marjoram and thyme are most approved) a tea spoon of cayenne, one pound butter, then dust with flour, then a layer of slices with slices of veal and seasoning till completed, cover with the liquor, stew gently three quarters of an hour. To make the forced meat balls—take one and half pound veal, one pound grated bread, 4 ounces raw salt pork, mince and season with above and work with 3 whites into balls, one or one an half inch diameter, roll in flour, and fry in very hot butter till brown, then chop the brains fine and stir into the whole mess in the pot, put thereto, one third part of the fried balls and a pint wine or less, when all is heated thro' take off and serve in tureens, laying the residue of the balls and hard boiled and peeled eggs into a dish, garnish with slices of lemon.

A Stew Pie.

Boil a shoulder of Veal, and cut up, salt, pepper, and butter half pound, and slices of raw salt pork, make a layer of meat, and a layer of biscuit, or biscuit dough into a pot, cover close and stew half an hour in three quarts of water only.

A Sea Pie.

Four pound of flour, one and half pound of butter rolled into paste, wet with cold water, line the pot therewith, lay in split pigeons, turkey pies, veal, mutton or birds, with slices of pork, salt, pepper, and dust on flour, doing thus till the pot is full or your ingredients expended, add three pints water, cover tight with paste, and stew moderately two and half hours.

A Chicken Pie.

Pick and clean six chickens, (without scalding) take out their inwards and wash the birds while whole, then joint the birds, salt and pepper the pieces and inwards. Roll one inch thick paste No. 8 and cover a deep dish, and double at the rim or edge of the dish, put thereto a layer of chickens and a layer of thin slices of butter, till the chickens and one and a half pound butter are expended, which cover with a thick paste; bake one and a half hour.

Or if your oven be poor, parboil the chickens with half a pound of butter, and put the pieces with the remaining one pound of butter, and half the gravy into the paste, and while boiling, thicken the residue of the gravy, and when the pie is drawn, open the crust, and add the gravy.

Minced Pies. A Foot Pie.

Scald neets feet, and clean well, (grass fed are best) put them into a large vessel of cold water, which change daily during a week, then boil the feet till tender, and take away the bones, when cold, chop fine, to every four pound minced meat, add one pound of beef suet, and four pound apple raw, and a little salt, chop all together very fine, add one quart of wine, two pound of stoned raisins, one ounce of cinnamon, one ounce mace, and sweeten to your taste; make use of paste No. 3—bake three quarters of an hour. Weeks after, when you have occasion to use them, carefully raise the top crust, and with a round edg'd spoon, collect the meat into a basin, which warm with additional wine and spices to the taste of your circle, while the crust is also warm'd like a hoe cake, put carefully together and serve up, by this means you can have hot pies through the winter, and enrich'd singly to your company.

Tongue Pie.

One pound neat's tongue, one pound apple, one third of a pound of Sugar, one quarter of a pound of butter, one pint of wine, one pound of raisins, or currants, (or half of each) half ounce of cinnamon and mace—bake in paste No. 1, in proportion to size.

Minced Pie of Beef.

Four pound boild beef, chopped fine, and salted; six pound of raw apple chopped also, one pound beef suet, one quart of Wine or rich sweet cider, one ounce mace, and cinnamon, a nutmeg, two pounds raisins, bake in paste No. 3, three fourths of an hour.

Observations.

All meat pies require a hotter and brisker oven than fruit pies, in good cookeries, all raisins should be stoned.—As people differ in their tastes, they may alter to their wishes. And as it is difficult to ascertain with precision the small articles of spicery; every one may relish as they like, and suit their taste.

Apple Pie.

Stew and strain the apples, to every three pints, grate the peel of a fresh lemon, add cinnamon, mace, rose-water and sugar to your taste—and bake in paste No. 3.

Every species of fruit such as peas, plums, raspberries, blackberries may be only sweetened, without spices—and bake in paste No. 3.

Currant Pies.

Take green, full grown currants, and one third their quantity of sugar, proceeding as above.

A buttered apple Pie.

Pare, quarter and core tart apples, lay in paste No. 3, cover with the same; bake half an hour, when drawn, gently raise the top crust, add sugar, butter, cinnamon, mace, and a sufficient quantity of wine or rose-water.

PUDDINGS.

A Rice Pudding.

One quarter of a pound rice, a stick of cinnamon, to a quart of milk (stirred often to keep from burning) and boil quick, cool and add half a nutmeg, 4 spoons rose-water, 8 eggs; butter or puff paste a dish and pour the above composition into it, and bake one and half hour.

No. 2. Boil 6 ounces rice in a quart milk, on a slow fire 'till tender, stir in one pound butter, interim beat 14 eggs, add to the pudding when cold with sugar, salt, rose-water and spices to your taste, adding raisins or currants, bake as No. 1.

No. 3. 8 spoons rice boiled in 2 quarts milk, when cooled add 8 eggs, 6 ounces butter, wine, sugar and spices, a sufficient quantity—bake 2 hours.

No. 4. Boil in water half pound ground rice till soft, add 2 quarts milk and scald, cool and add 8 eggs, 6 ounces butter, 1 pound raisins, salt, cinnamon and a small nutmeg, bake 2 hours.

No. 5. *A cheap one*, half pint rice, 2 quarts milk, salt, butter, allspice, put cold into a hot oven, bake 2 and half hours.

No. 6. Put 6 ounces rice into water, or milk and water, let it swell or soak tender, then boil gently, stirring in a little butter, when cool stir in a quart cream, 6 or 8 eggs well beaten, and add cinnamon, nutmeg, and sugar to your taste, bake.

N. B. The mode of introducing the ingredients, is a material point; in all cases where eggs are mentioned it is understood to be well beat; whites and yolks and the spices, fine and settled.

A Nice Indian Pudding.

No. 1. 3 pints scalded milk, 7 spoons fine Indian meal, stir well together while hot, let stand till cooled; add 7 eggs, half pound raisins, 4 ounces butter, spice and sugar, bake one and half hour.

No. 2. 3 pints scalded milk to one pint meal salted; cool, add 2 eggs, 4 ounces butter, sugar or molasses and spice sufficient, it will require two and half hours baking.

No. 3. Salt a pint meal, wet with one quart milk, sweeten and put into a strong cloth, brass or bell metal vessel, stone or earthen pot, secure from wet and boil 12 hours.

A Sunderland Pudding.

Whip 6 eggs, half the whites, take half a nutmeg, one point cream and a little salt, 4 spoons fine flour, oil or butter pans, cups, or bowls, bake in a quick oven one hour. Eat with sweet sauce.

A Whitpot.

Cut half a loaf of bread in slices, pour thereon 2 quarts milk, 6 eggs, rose-water, nutmeg and half pound of sugar; put into a dish and cover with paste, No. 1. bake slow 1 hour.

A Bread Pudding.

One pound soft bread or biscuit soaked in one quart milk, run thro' a sieve or colander, add 7 eggs, three quarters of a pound sugar, one quarter of a pound butter, nutmeg or cinnamon, one gill rose-water, one pound stoned raisins, half pint cream, bake three quarters of an hour, middling oven.

A Flour Pudding.

Seven eggs, one quarter of a pound of sugar, and a tea spoon of salt, beat and put to one quart milk, 5 spoons of flour, cinnamon and nutmeg to your taste, bake half an hour, and serve up with sweet sauce.

A boiled Flour Pudding.

One quart milk, 9 eggs, 7 spoons flour, a little salt. put into a strong cloth and boiled three quarters of an hour.

A Cream Almond Pudding.

Boil gently a little mace and half a nutmeg (grated) in a quart cream; when cool, beat 8 yolks and 3 whites, strain and mix with one spoon flour one quarter of a pound almonds; settled, add one spoon rose-water, and by degrees the cold cream and beat well together; wet a thick cloth and flour it, and pour in the pudding, boil hard half an hour, take out, pour over it melted butter and sugar.

An apple Pudding Dumplin.

Put into paste, quartered apples, lie in a cloth and boil two hours, serve with sweet sauce.

Pears, Plumbs, etc.,

Are done the same way.

Potato Pudding. Baked.

No. 1. One pound boiled potatoes, one pound sugar, half a pound butter, 10 eggs.

No. 2. One pound boiled potatoes, mashed, three quarters of a pound butter, 3 gills milk or cream, the juice of one lemon and the peel grated, half a pound sugar, half nutmeg, 7 eggs (taking out 3 whites,) 2 spoons rose-water.

Apple Pudding.

One pound apple sifted, one pound sugar, 9 eggs, one quarter of a pound butter, one quart sweet cream, one gill rose-water, a cinnamon, a green lemon peel grated (if sweet apples,) add the juice of half a lemon, put on to paste No. 7. Currants, raisins and citron some add, but good without them.

Carrot Pudding.

A coffee cup full of boiled and strained carrots, 5 eggs, 2 ounces sugar and butter each, cinnamon and rose-water to your taste, baked in a deep dish without paste.

A Crookneck, or Winter Squash Pudding.

Core, boil and skin a good squash, and bruise it well; take 6 large apples, pared, cored, and sewed tender, mix together; add 6 or 7 spoonsful of dry bread or biscuit, rendered fine as meal, half pint milk or cream, 2 spoons of rose-water, 2 do. wine, 5 or 6 eggs beaten and strained, nutmeg, salt and sugar to your taste, one spoon flour, beat all smartly together, bake.

The above is a good receipt for Pumpkins, Potatoes or Yams, adding more moistening or milk and rose-water, and to the two latter a few black or Lisbon currants, or dry whortleberries scattered in, will make it better.

Pumpkin.

No. 1. One quart stewed and strained, 3 pints cream, 9 beaten eggs, sugar, mace, nutmeg and ginger, laid into paste No. 7 or 3, and with a dough spur, cross and checker it, and baked in dishes three quarters of an hour.

No. 2. One quart of milk, 1 pint pumpkin, 4 eggs, molasses, allspice and ginger in a crust, bake 1 hour.

Orange Pudding.

Put sixteen yolks with half a pound butter melted, grate in the rinds of two Seville oranges, beat in half pound of fine Sugar, add two spoons orange water, two of rose-water, one gill of wine, half pint cream, two naples biscuit or the crumbs of a fine loaf, or roll soaked in cream, mix all together, put it into rich puff-paste, which let be double round the edges of the dish; bake like a custard.

A Lemon Pudding.

1. Grate the yellow of the peels of three lemons, then take two whole lemons, roll under your hand on the table till soft, taking care not to burst them, cut and squeeze them into the grated peels.

2. Take ten ounces soft wheat bread, and put a pint of scalded white wine thereto, let soak and put to No. 1.

3. Beat four whites and eight yolks, and put to above, adding three quarters of a pound of melted butter, (which let be very fresh and good) one pound fine sugar, beat all together till thoroughly mixed.

4. Lay paste No. 7 or 9 on a dish, plate or saucers, and fill with above composition.

5. Bake near 1 hour, and when baked—stick on pieces of paste, cut with a jagging iron or a dough-spur to your fancy, baked lightly on a floured paper; garnished thus, they may be served hot or cold.

Puff Pastes for Tarts.

No. 1. Rub one pound of butter into one pound of flour, whip 2 whites and add with cold water and one yolk; make into paste, roll in, in six or seven times one pound of butter, flouring it each roll. This is good for any small thing.

No. 2. Rub six pound of butter into fourteen pound of flour, eight eggs, add cold water, make a stiff paste.

No. 3. To any quantity of flour, rub in three fourths of it's weight of butter, (twelve eggs to a peck) rub in one third or half, and roll in the rest.

No. 4. Into two quarts flour (salted) and wet stiff with cold water roll in, in nine or ten times one and half pound of butter.

No. 5. One pound flour, three fourths of a pound of butter, beat well.

No. 6. To one pound of flour rub in one fourth of a pound of butter wet with three eggs and rolled in a half pound of butter.

A Paste for Sweet Meats.

No. 7. Rub one third of one pound of butter, and one pound of lard into two pound of flour, wet with four whites well beaten; water as much as necessary to make a paste, roll in the residue of shortening in ten or twelve rollings—bake quick.

No. 8. Rub in one and half pound of suet to six pounds of flour, and a spoon full of salt, wet with cream roll in, in six or eight times, two and half pounds of butter—good for a chicken or meat pie.

Royal Paste,

No. 9. Rub half a pound of butter into one pound of flour, four whites beat to a foam, add two yolks, two ounces of fine sugar; roll often, rubbing one third, and rolling two thirds of the butter is best; excellent for tarts and apple cakes.

CUSTARDS.

1. One pint cream sweetened to your taste, warmed hot; stir in sweet wine, till curdled, grate in cinnamon and nutmeg.

2. Sweeten a quart of milk, add nutmeg, wine, brandy, rose-water and six eggs; bake in tea cups or dishes, or boil in water, taking care that it don't boil into the cups.

3. Put a stick of cinnamon into one quart of milk, boil well, add six eggs, two spoons of rose-water—bake.

4. *Boiled Custard*—one pint of cream, two ounces of almonds, two spoons of rose-water, or orange flower water, some mace; boil thick, then stir in sweetening, and lade off into china cups, and serve up.

Rice Custard.

Boil a little mace, a quartered nutmeg in a quart of cream, add rice (well boiled) while boiling sweeten and flavor with orange or rose-water, putting into cups or dishes, when cooled, set to serve up.

A Rich Custard.

Four eggs beat and put into one quart cream, sweetened to your taste, half a nutmeg, and a little cinnamon—baked.

A sick bed Custard.

Scald a quart milk, sweeten and salt a little, whip 3 eggs and stir in, bake on coals in a pewter vessel.

TARTS.

Apple Tarts.

Stew and strain the apples, add cinnamon, rose-water, wine and sugar to your taste, lay in paste, royal, squeeze thereon orange juice—bake gently.

Cranberries.

Stewed, strained and sweetened, put into paste No. 9, and baked gently.

Marmalade, laid into paste No. 1, baked gently.

Apricots, must be neither pared, cut or stoned, but put in whole, and sugar sifted over them, as above.

Orange or Lemon Tart.

Take 6 large lemons, rub them well in salt, put them into salt and water and let rest 2 days, change them daily in fresh water, 14 days, then cut slices and mince as fine as you can and boil them 2 or 3 hours till tender, then take 6 pippins, pare, quarter and core them, boil in 1 pint fair water till the pippins break, then put the half of the pippins, with all the liquor to the orange or lemon, and add one pound sugar, boil all together one quarter of an hour, put into a gallipot and squeeze thereto a fresh orange, one spoon of which, with a spoon of the pulp of the pippin, laid into a thin royal paste, laid into small shallow pans or saucers, brushed with melted butter, and some superfine sugar sifted thereon, with a gentle baking, will be very good.

N. B. pastry pans, or saucers, must be buttered lightly before the paste is laid on. If glass or China be used, have only a top crust, you can garnish with cut paste, like a lemon pudding or serve on paste No. 7.

Gooseberry Tart.

Lay clean berries and sift over them sugar, then berries and sugar 'till a deep dish be filled, cover with paste No. 9, and bake some what more than other tarts.

Grapes, must be cut in two and stoned and done like a Gooseberry.

SYLLABUBS.

To make a fine Syllabub from the Cow.

Sweeten a quart of cider with double refined sugar, grate nutmeg into it, then milk your cow into your liquor, when you have thus added what quantity of milk you think proper, pour half a pint or more, in proportion to the quantity of syllabub you make, of the sweetest cream you can get all over it.

A Whipped Syllabub.

Take two porringers of cream and one of white wine, grate in the skin of a lemon, take the whites of three eggs, sweeten it to your taste, then whip it with a whisk, take off the froth as it rises and put it into your syllabub glasses or pots, and they are fit for use.

To make a fine Cream.

Take a pint of cream, sweeten it to your palate, grate a little nutmeg, put in a spoonful of orange flower water and rose-water, and two spoonfuls of wine; beat up four eggs and two whites, stir it all together one way over the fire till it is thick, have cups ready and pour it in.

Lemon Cream.

Take the juice of four large lemons, half a pint of water, a pound of double refined sugar beaten fine, the whites of seven eggs and the yolk of one beaten very well; mix altogether, strain it, set it on a gentle fire, stirring it all the while and skim it clean, put into it the peel of one lemon, when it is very hot, but not to boil; take out the lemon peel and pour it into china dishes.

Raspberry Cream.

Take a quart of thick sweet cream and boil it two or three wallops, then take it off the fire and strain some juices of raspberries into it to your taste, stir it a good while before you put your juice in, that it may be almost cold, when you put it to it, and afterwards stir it one way for almost a quarter of an hour; then sweeten it to your taste and when it is cold you may send it up.

Whipped Cream.

Take a quart of cream and the whites of 8 eggs beaten with half a pint of wine; mix it together and sweeten it to your taste with double refined sugar, you may perfume it (if you please) with musk or Amber gum tied in a rag and steeped a little in the cream, whip it up with a whisk and a bit of lemon peel tied in the middle of the whisk, take off the froth with a spoon, and put into glasses.

A Trifle.

Fill a dish with biscuit finely broken, rusk and spiced cake, wet with wine, then pour a good boil'd custard, (not too thick) over the rusk, and put a syllabub over that; garnish with jelly and flowers.

CAKE.

Plumb Cake.

Mix one pound currants, one drachm nutmeg, mace and cinnamon each, a little salt, one pound of citron, orange peel candied, and almonds bleach'd, 6 pound of flour, (well dried) beat 21 eggs, and add with 1 quart new ale yeast, half pint of wine, 3 half pints of cream and a sufficient quantity of raisins.

Plain Cake.

Nine pound of flour, 3 pound of sugar, 3 pound of butter, 1 quart emptins, 1 quart milk, 9 eggs, 1 ounce of spice, 1 gill of rose-water, 1 gill of wine.

Another.

Three quarters of a pound of sugar, 1 pound of butter, and 6 eggs work'd into 1 pound of flour.

A rich Cake.

Rub 2 pound of butter into 5 pound of flour, add 15 eggs (not much beaten) 1 pint of emptins, 1 pint of wine, kneed up stiff like biscuit, cover well and put by and let rise over night.

To 2 and a half pound raisins, add 1 gill brandy, to soak over night, or if new half an hour in the morning, add them with 1 gill rose-water and 2 and half pound of loaf sugar, 1 ounce cinnamon, work well and bake as loaf cake, No. 1.

Potato Cake.

Boil potatoes, peel and pound them, add yolks of eggs, wine and melted butter work with flour into paste, shape as you please, bake and pour over them melted butter, wine and sugar.

Johny Cake, or Hoe Cake.

Scald 1 pint of milk and put to 3 piats of indian meal, and half pint of flower—bake before the fire. Or scald with milk two thirds of the indian meal, or wet two thirds with boiling water, add salt, molasses and shortening, work up with cold water pretty stiff, and bake as above.

Indian Slapjack.

One quart of milk, 1 pint of indian meal, 4 eggs, 4 spoons of flour, little salt, beat together, baked on griddles, or fry in a dry pan, or baked in a pan which has been rub'd with suet, lard or butter.

Loaf Cakes.

No. 1. Rub 6 pound of sugar, 2 pound of lard, 3 pound of butter into 12 pound of flour, add 18 eggs, 1 quart of milk, 2 ounces of cinnamon, 2 small nutmegs, a tea cup of coriander seed, each pounded fine and sifted, add one pint of brandy, half a pint of wine, 6 pound of stoned raisins, 1 pint of emptins, first having dried your flour in the oven, dry and roll the sugar fine, rub your shortening and sugar half an hour, it will render the cake much whiter and lighter, heat the oven with dry wood, for 1 and a half hours, if large pans be used, it will then require 2 hours baking, and in proportion for smaller loaves. To frost it. Whip 6 whites, during the baking, add 3 pound of sifted loaf sugar and put on thick, as it comes hot from the oven. Some return the frosted loaf into the oven, it injures and yellows it, if the frosting be put on immediately it does best without being returned into the oven.

Another.

No. 2. Rub 4 pound of sugar, 3 and a half pound of shortening, (half butter and half lard) into 9 pound of flour, 1 dozen of eggs, 2 ounces of cinnamon 1 pint of milk, 3 spoonfuls coriander feed, 3 gills of brandy, 1 gill of wine, 3 gills of emptins, 4 pounds of raisins.

Another.

No. 3. Six pound of flour, 3 of sugar, 2 and a half pound of shortening, (half butter, half lard) 6 eggs, 1 nutmeg, 1 ounce of cinnamon and 1 ounce of coriander seed, 1 pint of emptins, 2 gills brandy, 1 pint of milk and 3 pound of raisins.

Another.

No. 4. Five pound of flour, 2 pound of butter, 2 and a half pounds of loaf sugar, 2 and a half pounds of raisins, 15 eggs, 1 pint of wine, 1 pint of emptins, 1 ounce of cinnamon, 1 gill rose-water, 1 gill of brandy—baked like No. 1.

Another Plain cake.

No. 5. Two quarts milk, 3 pound of sugar, 3 pound of shortning, warmed hot, add a quart of sweet cider, this curdle, add 18 eggs, allspice and orange to your taste, or fennel, carroway or coriander seeds; put to 9 pounds of flour, 3 pints emptins, and bake well.

Cookies.

One pound sugar boiled slowly in half pint water, scum well and cool, add two tea spoons pearl ash dissolved in milk, then two and half pounds flour, rub in 4 ounces butter, and two large spoons of finely powdered coriander seed, wet with above; make rolls half an inch thick and cut to the shape you please; bake fifteen or twenty minutes in a slack oven—good three weeks.

Another *Christmas Cookie.*

To three pound flour, sprinkle a tea cup of fine powdered coriander seed, rub in one pound butter, and one and half pound sugar, dissolve three tea spoonfuls of pearl ash in a tea cup of milk, kneed all together well, roll three quarters of an inch thick, and cut or stamp into shape and size you please, bake slowly fifteen or twenty minutes; tho' hard and dry at first, if put into an earthen pot, and dry cellar, or damp room, they will be finer, softer and better when six months old.

Molasses Gingerbread.

One table spoon of cinnamon, some coriander or allspice, put to four tea spoons pearl ash, dissolved in half pint water, four pound flour, one quart molasses, four ounces butter, (if in summer rub in the butter, if in winter, warm the butter and molasses and pour to the spiced flour,) knead well 'till stiff, the more the better, the lighter and whiter it will be; bake brisk fifteen minutes; don't scorch; before it is put in, wash it with whites and sugar beat together.

Gingerbread Cakes, or butter and sugar Gingerbread.

No. 1. Three pounds of flour, a grated nutmeg, two ounces ginger, one pound sugar, three small spoons pearl ash dissolved in cream, one pound butter, four eggs, knead it stiff, shape it to your fancy, bake 15 minutes.

Soft Gingerbread to be baked in pans.

No. 2. Rub three pounds of sugar, two pounds of butter, into four pounds of flour, add 20 eggs, 4 ounces ginger, 4 spoons rose-water, bake as No. 1.

Butter drop do.

No. 3. Rub one quarter of a pound butter, one pound sugar, sprinkled with mace, into one pound and a quarter flour, add four eggs, one glass rose-water, bake as No. 1.

Gingerbread.

No. 4. Three pound sugar, half pound butter, quarter of a pound of ginger, one doz. eggs, one glass rose-water, rub into three pounds flour, bake as No. 1.